Am I Democrat or Republican?
Political Affiliation Test

by JEST FEST

DISCLAIMER: The results achieved from the activities in this book have not been clinically proven or evaluated by the FDA, EPA, WHO, NWO or the Illuminati. For professional advice, please consult your local Flat Earth Society.

*"You can always count on Americans
to do the right thing –
after they have tried everything else."*

Winston Churchill

This paperback edition first published
in 2020 by Dialog Abroad Books.

Copyright © Jest Fest, 2020.

2   4   6   8   10   9   7   5   3   1

ISBN: 978-3-948706-53-1

THE INNARDS

PART 2: THE ANSWERS

PART 3: THE RESULTS

BONUS: BADGES
I'm a Democrat
I'm a Republican

MORE FROM JEST FEST

PART 1: The TEST

Hot or Not

Politics ain't pretty. But some politicians are. Compare the photos below and choose who you think is the better looking male and female politician. Circle only 1 letter and 1 number.

A.

B.

1.

2.

Hell to the Yeah/Naw!

For each of the 3 sections, draw a line to connect the words on the left to one of the words on the right.

A.

Guns   Hell yeah!

Weed   Hell naw!

- - - - -

B.

God   Hell yeah!

Science   Hell naw!

- - - - -

C.

FOX   Hell yeah!

CNN   Hell naw!

Blitz Maze

Quickly and without thinking, select and trace a dotted line A, B or C along the path to reveal which of these three NFL teams your subconscious mind supports.

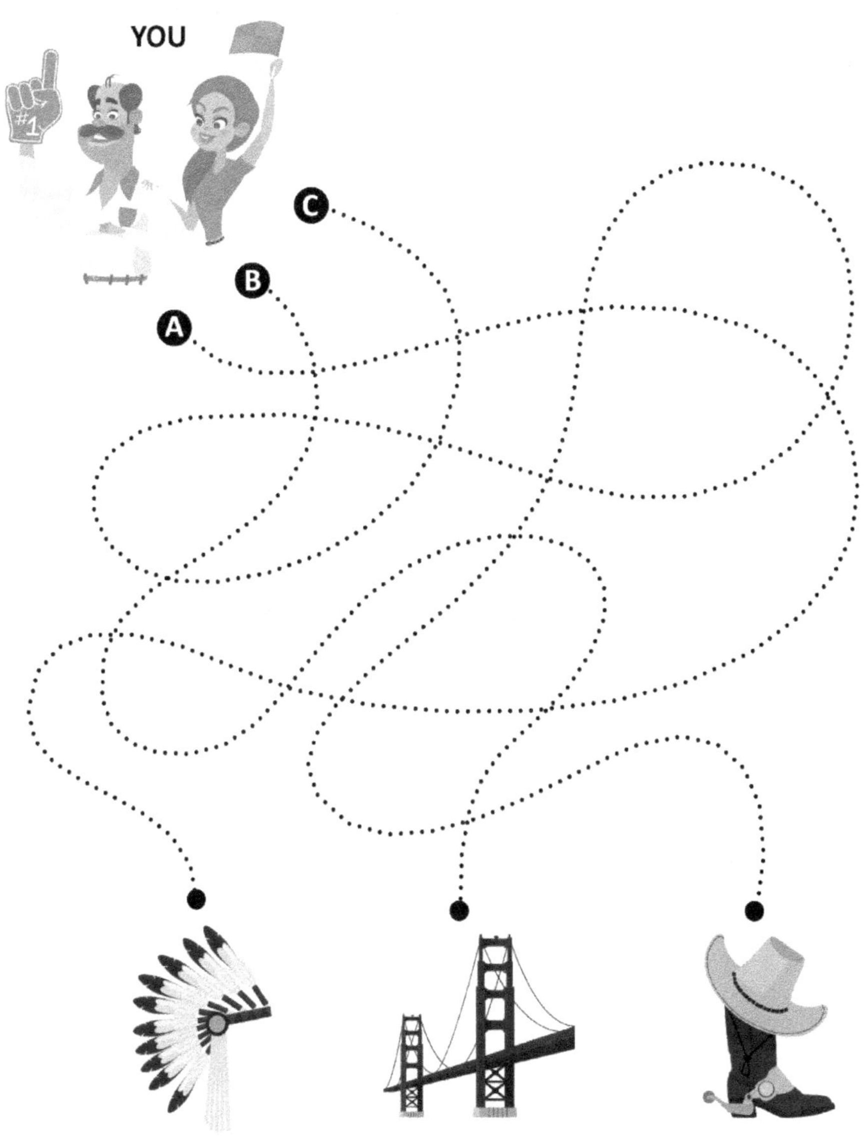

Guess the Movie Quote

Guess which movies the following quotes came from.

A: "Incompetence is often highly regarded in governmental circles." (1995)

Movie: _______________________

B: "Well, well, well. I'd say diplomacy has failed." (2009)

Movie: _______________________

C: "Why is it when your life exceeds your wildest dreams, a knife appears at your back?" (2011)

Movie: _______________________

Animal Hunter

Six animals are hidden below. Circle the <u>first three</u> animals you see.

Partisanagram

The following phrases will reveal the names of celebrity democrats and republicans. Which one will you complete <u>first</u>?

Major lass in heat!

Answer: ________________________________

A firearm career!

Answer: ________________________________

He's grown large 'n' crazed!

Answer: ________________________________

A periodical donor!

Answer: ________________________________

Turning Pro

American parents are obsessed with their children being good at sports. But what sport do you want your kid to grow up playing and possibly turning pro? Circle one of the sports below.

Number Puzzle Picture

In any order you wish, copy the contents of each square in the jumbled picture below to the same numbered square in the blank grid on the next page until the entire puzzle is done, and then complete the phrase describing the completed picture.

This is a picture of a _______________________________.

Fill in the Blank Song Lyrics

Fill in the missing word in the following song lyrics.

A:

"You remember the night that you left me
You put me in my place
Got you in a ________________ baby
You're gone, I crushed your face."

- - - - -

B:

"Take my hand, stay ______________
Heaven's not ready for you
Every part of my aching heart
Needs you more than the angels do."

Brand Wordsearch

Circle the first two brand names you see. <u>Only circle two</u>.

I N D O C T R I N A T I O N
I N D O C T R I N A T I O N
I N D O C T R I N A T I O N
I N D O C T K I N A T I O N
I N D O C T R E N A T I O N
I N D O C T R I L A T I O N
I N D O C T R I J L T I O N
I N D O C T R A N A O I O N
I N D O C T X I N A T G O N
I N D O C T R I N A T I G N
I N D O C T R I N A T I O S
I N D O C T R I N A T I O N
I N D O C T R I N A T I O N
I I D O C T R A M S T E P N
I K D O C T R I N A T I O N
I E D O C T R I N A T I O N

Rainbowtically Correct

Label each stripe in the LGBT Pride Day flag.

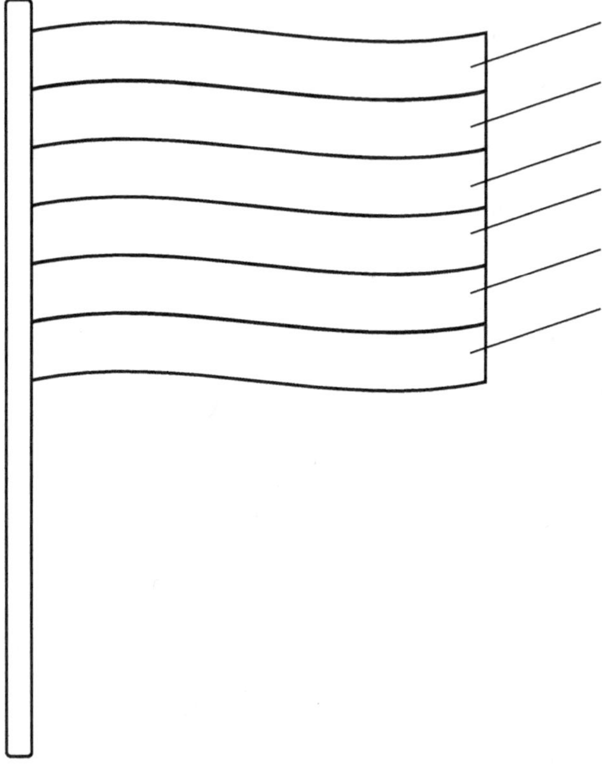

Subliminal Sudoku

Fill in the blank squares so that each row, each column, and each
3-by-3 block contain all the letters A, B, C, D, E, G, O, S, T.

The first word you produce from one of the two highlighted sections will be
used to complete the following phrase to describe you:

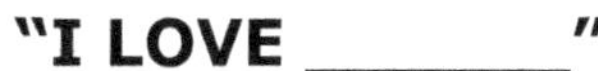

"I LOVE _______"

D	T	O				G		E
			D				B	T
	S		T	E	G			
O	D					B		
	B	T	C		E	A	S	
		E					C	D
			G	C	T	E	D	A
E	G				O			
T		A						S

PART 2: The ANSWERS

Hot or Not

Politics ain't pretty. But some politicians are. Compare the photos below and choose the best-looking male and beautiful female politicians. Circle only 1 letter and 1 number.

A. 

B.

1. 

2.

If you circled:

- A & 2   = 0 points
- B & 1   = 5 points
- Any other combination   = 3 points

Points this round	
Total points so far	

Hell to the Yeah/Naw!

For each of the 3 sections, draw a line to connect the words on the left to one of the words on the right.

A.

      Guns   Hell yeah!

      Weed   Hell naw!

- - - - -

B.

      God   Hell yeah!

      Science   Hell naw!

- - - - -

C.

      FOX   Hell yeah!

      CNN   Hell naw!

If you completed the sections with:
- Crossed lines   = 0 points
- Parallel lines   = 5 points
- Any other combination   = 3 points

Points this round	
Total points so far	

Blitz Maze

Quickly and without thinking, select and trace a dotted line A, B or C along the path to reveal which of these three NFL teams your subconscious mind supports.

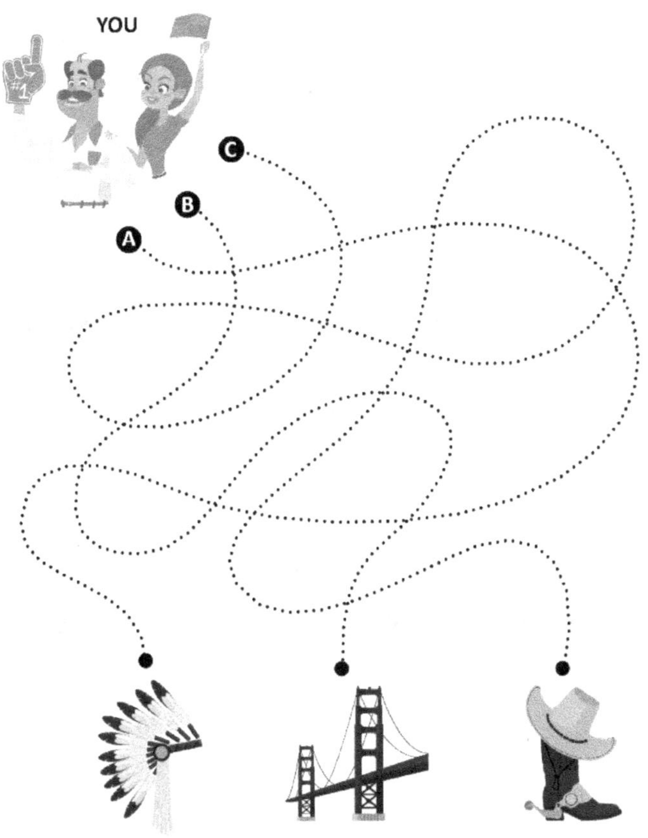

If you chose: **A** = 3 points **B** = 0 points **C** = 5 points
(Washington) (San Francisco) (Dallas)

Points in this round	
Total points so far	

Guess the Movie Quote

Guess which movies the following quotes came from.

A: *"Incompetence is often highly regarded in governmental circles."*

Movie: Braveheart (1995)

B: *"Well, well, well. I'd say diplomacy has failed."*

Movie: Avatar (2009)

C: *"Why is it when your life exceeds your wildest dreams, a knife appears at your back?"*

Movie: Limitless (2011)

If you answered:
- A correct, B+C incorrect or unanswered   = 5 points
- B correct, A+C incorrect or unanswered   = 0 points
- Any other combination   = 3 points

Points this round	
Total points so far	

Animal Hunter

Six animals are hidden below. Circle the <u>first three</u> animals you see.

If you circled:
- Cat, penguin, and donkey   = 0 points
- Dog, eagle, and elephant   = 5 points
- Any other combination   = 3 points

Points this round	
Total points so far	

Partisanagram

The following phrases will reveal the names of celebrity democrats and republicans. Which one will you complete <u>first</u>?

Major lass in heat!

Answer: <u>Melissa Joan Hart</u>

A firearm career!

Answer: <u>America Ferrera</u>

He's grown large 'n' crazed!

Answer: <u>Arnold Schwarzenegger</u>

A periodical donor!

Answer: <u>Leonardo DiCaprio</u>

If you wrote (points awarded for name you completed <u>first</u>):
- America Ferrera or Leonardo DiCaprio   = 0 points
- Melissa Joan Hart or Arnold Schwarzenegger   = 5 points
- All incorrect or unanswered   = 3 points

Points in this round	
Total points so far	

Turning Pro

American parents are obsessed with their children being good at sports. But what sport do you want your kid to grow up playing and possibly turning pro? Circle one of the sports below.

If you circled:

- Tennis or Soccer   = 0 points
- Baseball or Football   = 3 points
- Golf or Ice Hockey   = 5 points

Points this round	
Total points so far	

Number Puzzle Picture

In any order you wish, copy the contents of each square in the jumbled picture to the same numbered square in the blank grid until the entire puzzle is done, and then describe what you see in the completed picture.

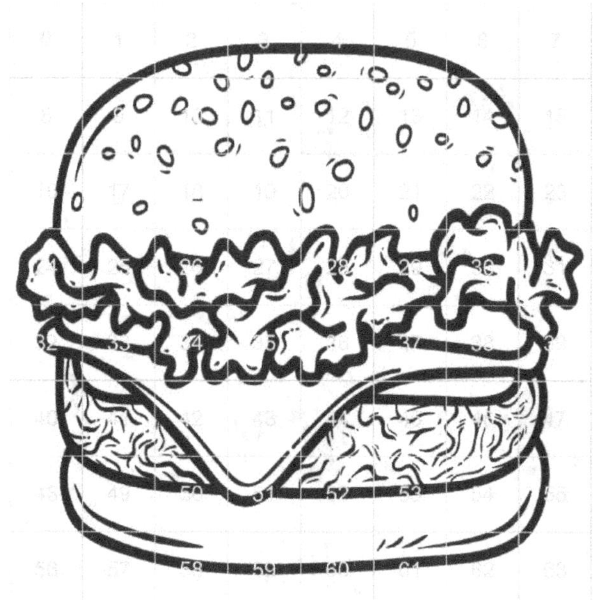

This is a picture of a _________________________.

If you wrote:

- Veggie burger (or similar)   = 0 points
- Hamburger (or similar)   = 5 points
- Any other answer   = 3 points

Points this round	
Total points so far	

Fill in the Blank Song Lyrics

Fill in the missing word in the following song lyrics.

A: (Ted Nugent, Stranglehold)

"You remember the night that you left me
You put me in my place
Got you in a <u>stranglehold</u> baby
You're gone, I crushed your face."

- - - - -

B: (Lady Gaga, Joanne)

"Take my hand, stay <u>Joanne</u>
Heaven's not ready for you
Every part of my aching heart
Needs you more than the angels do."

If you answered:
- A correct, B incorrect or unanswered   = 5 points
- B correct, A incorrect or unanswered   = 0 points
- Both correct or both incorrect or unanswered   = 3 points

Points this round	
Total points so far	

Brand Wordsearch

Circle the first two brand names you see. <u>Only circle two</u>.

```
I   N   D   O   C   T   R   I   N   A   T   I   O   N
I   N   D   O   C   T   R   I   N   A   T   I   O   N
I   N   D   O   C   T   R   I   N   A   T   I   O   N
I   N   D   O   C   T   K   I   N   A   T   I   O   N
I   N   D   O   C   T   R   E   N   A   T   I   O   N
I   N   D   O   C   T   R   I   L   A   T   I   O   N
I   N   D   O   C   T   R   I   J   L   T   I   O   N
I   N   D   O   C   T   R   A   N   A   O   I   O   N
I   N   D   O   C   T   X   I   N   A   T   G   O   N
I   N   D   O   C   T   R   I   N   A   T   I   G   N
I   N   D   O   C   T   R   I   N   A   T   I   O   S
I   N   D   O   C   T   R   I   N   A   T   I   O   N
I   N   D   O   C   T   R   I   N   A   T   I   O   N
I   I   D   O   C   T   R   A   M   S   T   E   P   N
I   K   D   O   C   T   R   I   N   A   T   I   O   N
I   E   D   O   C   T   R   I   N   A   T   I   O   N
```

If you circled:
- **NIKE** and **PETSMART**   = 5 points
- **KELLOGGS** and **AJAX**   = 0 points
- Any other words or combination = 3 points

Points in this round	
Total points so far	

Rainbowtically Correct

Label each stripe in the LGBT Pride Day flag.

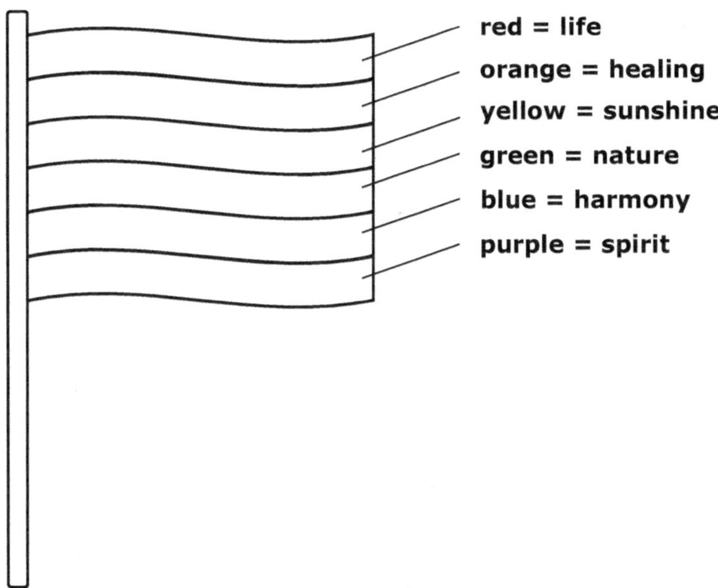

If you wrote:
- Colors and/or meanings in correct order = 0 points
- Any other answer = 5 points

Points this round	
Total points so far	

Subliminal Sudoku

Fill in the blank squares so that each row, each column, and each
3-by-3 block contain all the letters A, B, C, D, E, G, O, S, T.

The first word you produce from one of the two highlighted sections will be
used to complete the following phrase to describe you:

"I LOVE ________"

D	T	O	B	S	C	G	A	E
C	E	G	D	O	A	S	B	T
A	S	B	T	E	G	D	O	C
O	D	C	A	T	S	B	E	G
G	B	T	C	D	E	A	S	O
S	A	E	O	G	B	T	C	D
B	O	S	G	C	T	E	D	A
E	G	D	S	A	O	C	T	B
T	C	A	E	B	D	O	G	S

If you completed the phrase as (points awarded for the section you
completed <u>first</u>):

- **I LOVE CATS**   = 0 points
- **I LOVE DOGS**   = 5 points

Points this round	
TOTAL POINTS	

PART 3: The RESULTS

Total Points	Where you are on the political affiliation spectrum
0-12	You're a full-blown Democrat! You demand gun control, universal healthcare, and a shiny gold participation medal for your child despite her team's humiliating defeat.
13-24	You lean more to the left, having voted democrat since your Ivy League college days. Still, you see the prices at Wal-Mart compared to Whole Foods Market and think the conservatives might be onto something.
25-36	Left, right, blue, red, LGBT, NRA, whatever! As long as there's beer and nobody gets hurt, then anything goes for you and you don't care who knows it.
37-48	You lean more to the right, having voted republican since believing Saddam had WMDs. Still, you see how good your butt looks in Levi's compared to your Wranglers and think the liberals might be onto something.
49-60	You're a full-blown Republican! You demand increased military spending, abortion restrictions, and deportation of illegal immigrants (except your nanny and gardener!).

You may be asking:
- *Why do I get 3 points if I follow the NFL maze path to Washington?*
- *Why is tennis worth 0 points while golf is worth 5 points?*
- *And so on…*

The answers to such questions are extremely complex and open to a certain degree of interpretation. Perhaps, the best idea would be to express your bamboozlement with friends, social groups online, your psychotherapist, or even as part of your review of this book for others to help you muse, mull over and meditate upon the solutions.

BONUS: Badges

To make your test results even more special, here are two exclusive and exquisite badges for you to color in, cut out, and display with pride.

Go on... let everyone know just how much of a Democrat/Republican (delete as necessary) you really are!

I'm a Democrat

I'm a Republican

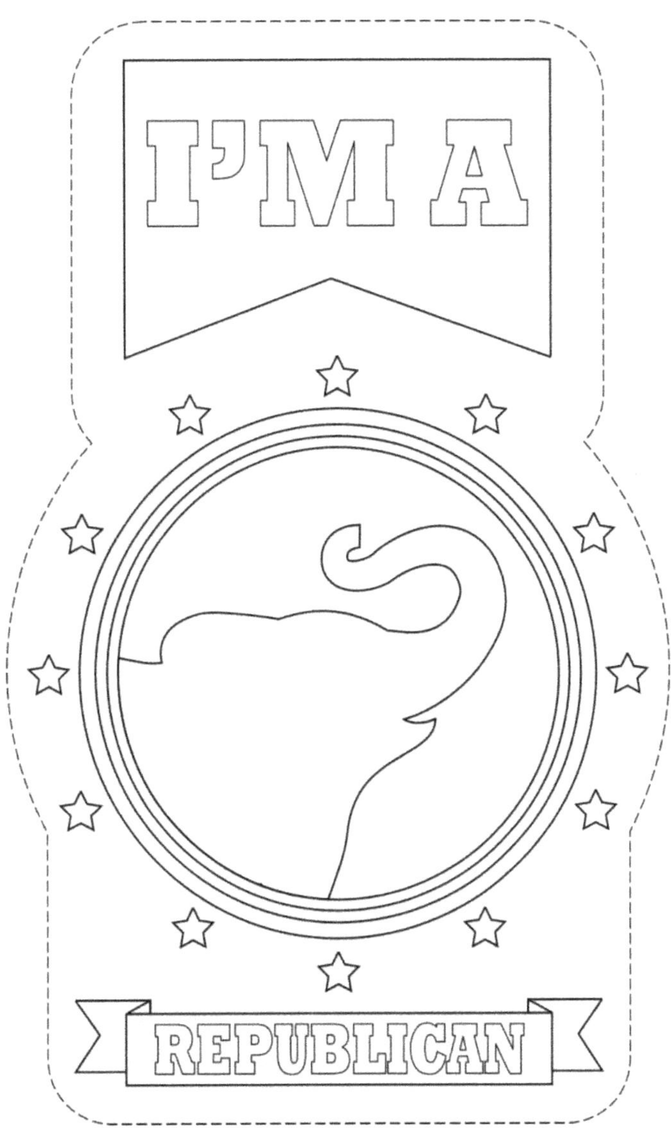

More From JEST FEST

Well, I hope this book made you laugh.

If you want more giggle-inspiring books to lighten the mood, I've got you covered.

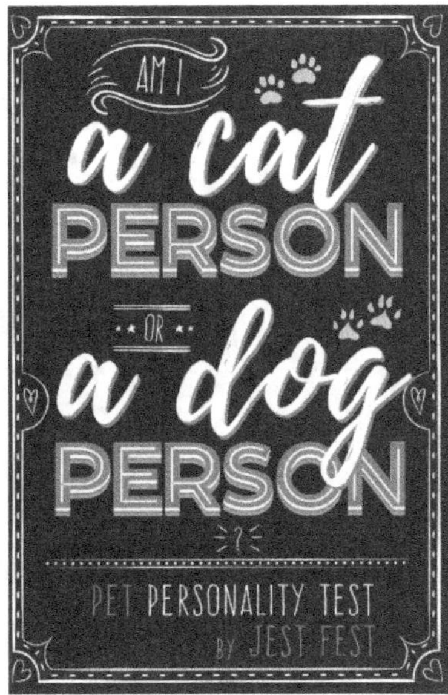